Sci-Fi
WESTERN

Art Show
111 Minna Gallery
San Francisco
January 23, 2003

CURATOR: SUNNY BUICK

Sci-Fi Western
A Catalog of 93 Artists Presented by
111 Minna Gallery of San Francisco
in Conjunction with the Gallery Show
January 23, 2003
Eiming Jung Proprieter
Published by
Last Gasp of San Francisco
777 Florida Street
San Francisco, CA 94110

Title © 2002 Sunny Buick
Book Copyright © 2002 Last Gasp
All Art Copyright © various artists
Cover Design by Alethea Morrison
Designed by Sasha Wingate
Front Cover Art by Todd Schorr
Back Cover Art by Douglas Fraser
Back Cover Pattern by Jim "Shift E" Breazeale
Title Page Art by KRK Ryden
Table of Contents Art by Tex
Foreword and Introduction Art by Ludovic Joffrain
Thank You Art by Sunny Buick

Curated and Conceived by Sunny Buick
www.sunnybuick.com
Introduction © 2002 John Clute

ISBN 0-86719-560-6
additional copies $30.- postpaid to our address, or order online at
www.lastgasp.com

Printed in Hong Kong by Prolong Press Limited

Table of Contents

Foreword

I've always been a girl with one eye on the past and the other winking at the future. As a child, I sat Indian-style in the dark too close to the television. My face glowed eerily from the flickering light. Westerns had little to offer a girl but beautiful horses and fancy clothes. Science fiction films, on the other hand, with their flashy destruction and glittering metallic surfaces captured my imagination. I spent hour after hour watching Roy Rogers and John Wayne, Godzilla and Flash Gordon. My flaky babysitter didn't bother to try to get me to bed on time.

Years later after having collected a vast number of artist friends, I formulated a strange vision. The combination of SCI/FI Western is not a new idea. It has been a part of the collective unconscious for quite some time. Yet there are few examples of this hybrid from the heyday of the two greatest B-movie genres. It would have been extremely difficult to present one film that would bring the two fan bases together. The incongruent time element and the fact that you were either a Science Fiction fan or a cowboy western fan posed the biggest problem. However why it never happened is puzzling, as the two subjects shared so many basic elements, good guys vs. bad guys, often a hero repelling a foreign force, with good always triumphing over evil. Desert landscapes whether on earth or in space set the stage for exploration, freedom and adventure. There were even symmetrical accessories, handguns and ray guns, coordinated uniforms and personified transportation. Maybe we weren't quite ready for our past to be introduced to our future. We were still trying to figure out what it all meant. Since those days Aliens, Indians, Cowboys, Spaceships, Robots and Rockets have become symbols and icons of America, an ideal America with a strong connection to yesteryears and a glorious vision of tomorrowland.

Why Science Fiction and Westerns? It is our own interpretation, personal myth and pure fantasy about our past and future. Each opened a world of possibilities, we imagined Time machines that would help us undo our errors and we imagined Space machines that would solve all the world's problems. Who lives in the present? No one. We're always holding on to an illusion of our glory days or residing in a dreamland of future utopias. The uncharted territory of the mind can be as lonely as the desert or space, chained to mistakes of yesterday or terrified of t shadowy nightmare of tomorrow. We struggle to ma sense of the two. In searching our hopes and fears uncover treasures in memories and the lessons learne With this knowledge we create the future through c dreams and imagination.

In SCI/FI Western we bring together yesterday and tom row. When the past and future are united we find t present. An artist lives in the present during the proce of making art. We solve each problem as it comes up a the proof is in the finished product. This theme inspir scores of creative geniuses to create a new vision esp cially for this show. It seems that Science/Fiction a Westerns were very important symbolically in our form tive years. When looking at this imagery it is interesting see who is winning in each artist's battle. In some of t pieces the future is horribly scary and in others it is hop ful and bright. How much does this reveal about our int nal landscapes? Within these pages we have visionari borrowing images of the past and leaving it to future ge erations to interpret where we were in this prese moment. Ladies and Gentlemen, through time warps a deadlines, showdowns and shootouts we bring to you t greatest collection of SCI/Fi Western Art ever presente Blast off, Partner!

Space Commander,
Sunny Buick
San Francisco
Planet Earth
01/03

Introduction

By John Clute

There's something wrong here, and there's something very right. Let's start with what is right. Over and above the quality of the works on show, over and above the professional pizzazz of the exhibition, which is obvious, there's something else that's very right, too. And that's the iconology of the thing. As Sunny Buick says in her introduction, the basic gear of the Western deserts, false-front frontier towns, saloons, guns, heroes, horses, uniforms is deeply similar to the basic gear of the space opera form of science fiction. For deserts read space, for deceptive frontier towns read planets, and for saloons read saloons. This is right, and this is good.

It's good because, for Western and space opera both, it works. Classic Westerns and space operas share, some very basic elements: romantic arenas in which actions are highly visible; conflicts between good and evil in which, almost always, the good hero stands alone (or with a band of brave Companions, who tag along like Seven Samurai) against an organized, corporate, exploitative foe; clear-cut outcomes, in which the bad are genuinely defeated, and the good complete their tasks without tarnish; and return. Westerns and space operas, at this basic level, are timeless. They tell primal tales which can be retold. We return to them, again and again, as open to wonder as children.

This is all well and good, and those works in this show devoted to illustrations that play on the pun of crossover make good fun and are good examples. But the greatest art comes out of wrongness, which is another way of saying that great art always threatens us by making something real that we never previously thought could ever be thought of as real. The works in this show that illuminate the wrongness of the conjunction of Western and space opera are, perhaps, even more interesting to contemplate than the technical goodness of the work Sunny Buick has assembled.

Great space operas are great, at least in part, because they threaten us by contradicting their model. Any Western written after (say) World War Two inhabits a polder, a term we used in The Encyclopedia of Fantasy (St Martin's, 1997) to define a protected, walled-in region of the world or of the mind where reality was more intense and pure than outside the walls, where princesses and heroes and mages could still do their stuff, where time stood still. Any post-War Western worth its salt, it seems to me, works as a doomed defense of polder. I think of almost any Western by John Ford; I think of True Grit, book and film; of Little Big Man, book and film; of Clint Eastwood's extreme Westerns, like the two supernaturals (High Plains Drifter and "Pale Rider"), and the great Unforgiven. It is books and movies like this that run-of-the-mill space operas ignore; it is books and movies like this that great space operas carry in their hearts.

Because great space operas (such as Dan Simmons's Hyperion Cantos) are not just about the arena of joy, where great stories can repeat in Paradise, even though they are set in the universe whose frontiers cannot be guessed. They are also about ending, about the erosion of the polder, the aging of the hero, the terrible side effects of vigorous action, the death of the West.

But always, in the great Westerns and in the great space operas which remember them, when the truth seems most terrible to bear and the story has no continuing, there is a gleam, the flash of teeth in a smile at dawn, and something next begins to happen. As the works on show here demonstrate, what unites the Western and the space opera, in the end, is the ray of hope.

Clayton Brothers "Howdy! My name is JIM"
11.25" x 13" Mixed Media, 2002

Ryan Kelly "The Day I Met H. G. Wells"
12" x 16" Acrylic on Canvas, 2002

Clayton Brothers "We
12" x 12" Mixed Media, 20

Mike Davis "Foreign Shores"
20.5" x 35" Acrylic on Wood, 2002

Mike Davis "Alpha Omega"
44.5" x 51.5" Acrylic on Wood, 2002

Mike Davis "The Spoils of War"
19.5" x 23.5" Acrylic on Wood, 2002

Mike Davis "An Eye for An Eye"
62" x 43.5" Acrylic on Wood, 2002

©ALMERA

Marco Almera "Space Cowgirl"
30" x 48" Acrylic on Canvas, 2002

Carson "Chile Con Carne"
24" x 12" Acrylic on Canvas, 2002

Carson "The Last Stand at Alien Gulch"
24" X 12" Acrylic on Canvas, 2002

Shaunna Peterson "Atomo Cheesecake: Girl with Gun"
27" x 16" Acrylic on Wood, 2002

Rachel Bickley "Rustic Space Container"
10.75" x 6.5" x 6" Enamel and Acrylic on Wooden Box, with Polymer Clay Accents, 2002

Gary Baseman "Space Cactus"
11" x 15" Acrylic, 2002

Hungry Dog Studio, Bob and Val Tillery "Cattle Mutilations: Circa 1880"
16" x 10" Mixed Media, 2002

Ron English "Alien Cowboy Clown"
24" x 16" Oil on canvas, 2002

Graham Chaffee "Astounding Western Tales #1"
12" x 17" Oil on Illustration Board, 2002

Adam Cruz "Coin-op Kiddie Ride"
8" x 12" Oil on Masonite, 2002

Rick Potts "Goin' To See A Man About A Horse"
12" x 14" x 11" Mixed Media, 2002

Jim Bauer "Untitled"
8" x 20" Mixed Media, 2002

Bosko "Happy Hour"
19" x 14" x 15" Mixed Media, 2002

Tom Williams "One Mile Inn"
40" x 24" Acrylic on Canvas, 2002

Winston Smith "Rodeo of Tomorrow"
10" x 13" Montage, 1999

James K. Wong "Moon Rockin"
16" x 20" Oil on Panel, 2002

Robert Williams "Mathematics Takes a Holiday"
36" x 32" Wasserman Silkscreen Print, 1991

Robert Williams "Cowboys and Amoebas"
21.5" x 18" Lithograph Print, 1992

Van Arno "Drumstick Sally"
20" x 32" Egg Tempura on Panel, 2002

Douglas Fraser "Dead Astronaut"
18" x 14" Alkyds on Masonite, 2002

Krystine Kryttre "Greetings From the Nevada Desert"
14" x 18" Acrylic on Board, 2002

Tex "Space Meanie Cowgirl"
11" x 15" Watercolor, 2002

Tex "Space Cutie Cowgirl"
11" x 15" Watercolor, 2002

Paul Valadez "Flying Saucer"
22" x 30" Acrylic on Paper, 2002

Joe Newton "Lunar Matinee"
36" x 49" Metallic Enamel and Automotive Primer, 2002

Ity "Sci/Firecracker Western"
Media, 2002

Jesus Angel "Txutxo" Perez "Untitled"
12" x 16" Silkscreen on Canvas, 2002

Rafael Lopez "Howdy Ma'am"
11" x 14" Acrylic on Wood, 2002

Jill Jordan "Rocket Maiden"
14" x 11" Watercolor on Paper, 2002

Anthony Ausgang "Come Back Soon Now, Y'hear!"
18" x 14" Acrylic on Found Canvas, 2002

Rocco "Midnight Rider"
53" x 40" Acrylic and Vinyl Acrylic on Canvas and Luan Board, 2002

Moritz R. "Texas Planet"
26" x 36" Oil on Canvas, 2002

Jim "Shift E" Breazeale "Untitled"
20" x 16" Digital Mixed Media, 2002

Jeral Tidwell "The Abduction of Lightning Jack"
12" x 46" Acrylic on Wood, 2002

Eric White "The Sheriff"
12" x 12" Oil on Wood, 2001

Mike Sosnowski "Shock Showdown"
36" x 24" Oil on Canvas, 2002

41

Sandra Equihua "Happy Trails"
9" x 8" Acrylic on Canvas, 2002

Kevin Scalzo "Kute Kowboy Kid"
16" x 16" Acrylic and Enamel on Wood, 2002

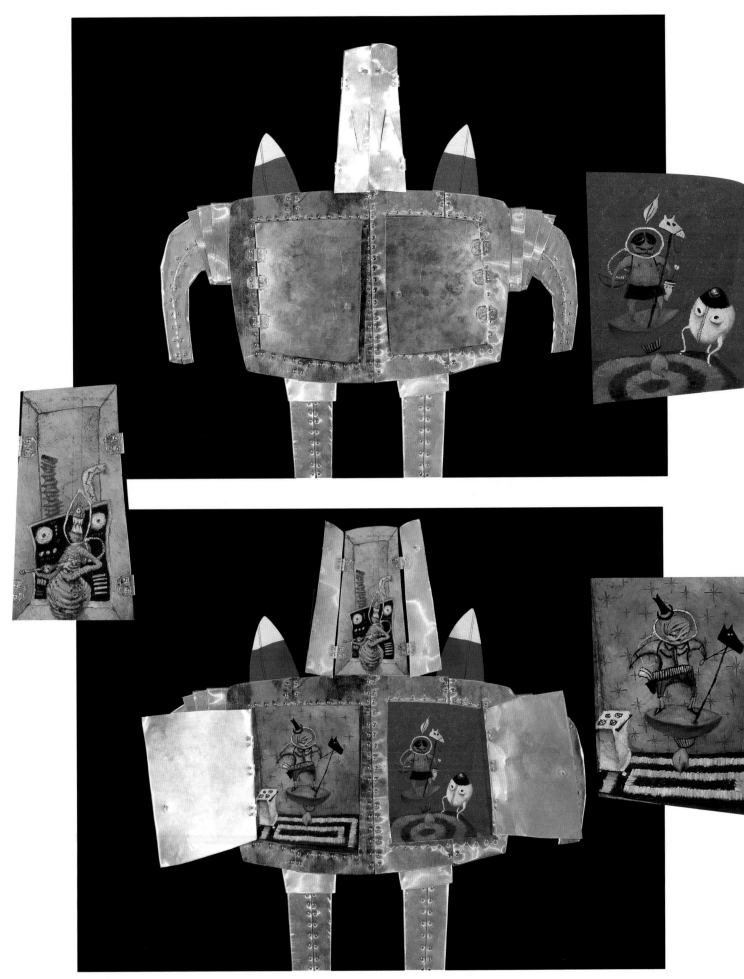

Johnny Dismal "JD27"
22" x 22" Oil, Wood, Tin, 2002

Lois Anderson "Up At The Ranch"
10" x 18" Mixed Media, 2002

Tara McPherson "Ace And Ion Go Space Mining"
19" x 15" Acrylic and Oil on Wood, 2002

Seonna Hong "Hopi He Doesn't Find Out"
6" x 8" Gouache on Paper, 2002

Sunny Buick
"The Love Machine"
84" x 60"
Acrylic on Canvas
2002

48

Tim Biskup "Round-up To Infinity"
11" x 15" Gouache on Wood, 2002

Kathy Schorr "Bubble Cat Roundup"
11" x 14" Oil on Board, 2002

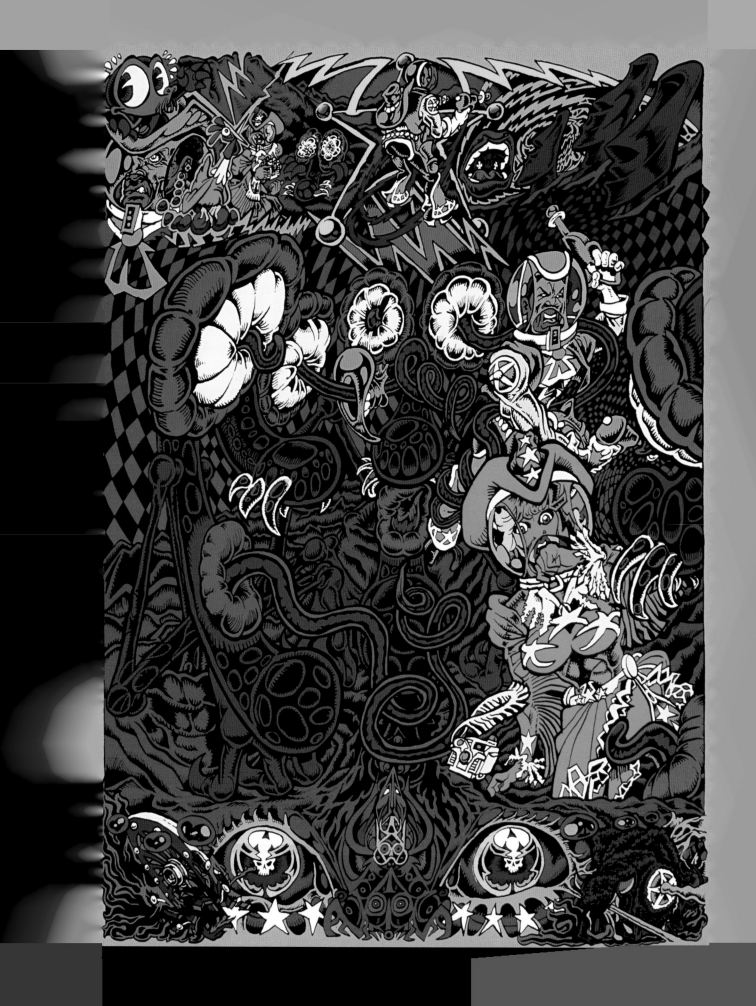

Ludovic Joffrain "Sci-Fi Western, One Vision"
29.7 x 42 centimeters Chromalin, 2002

Andrew Brandou "The Hunter"
7" x 5" Gouache on Wood, 2002

Andrew Brandou "The Butcher"
7" x 5" Gouache on Wood, 2002

Lisa Petrucci "Kosmic Kuties"
8" x 5" Acrylic, Varnish on Wood, 2002

Bwana Spoons "Muddy Rainbow Is That Way"
36" x 21" Acrylic on Metal, 2002

Al Cintraleite "Untitled"
8" x 10" Oil on Canvas Board, 2002

KEPI "Sundown #1"
6" x 12" Acrylic on Canvas, 2002

KEPI "Sundown #2"
6" x 12" Acrylic on Canvas, 2002

Vicki M. "Corporate Cowboy Wallpaper"
12" x 12" Acrylic on Canvas, 2002

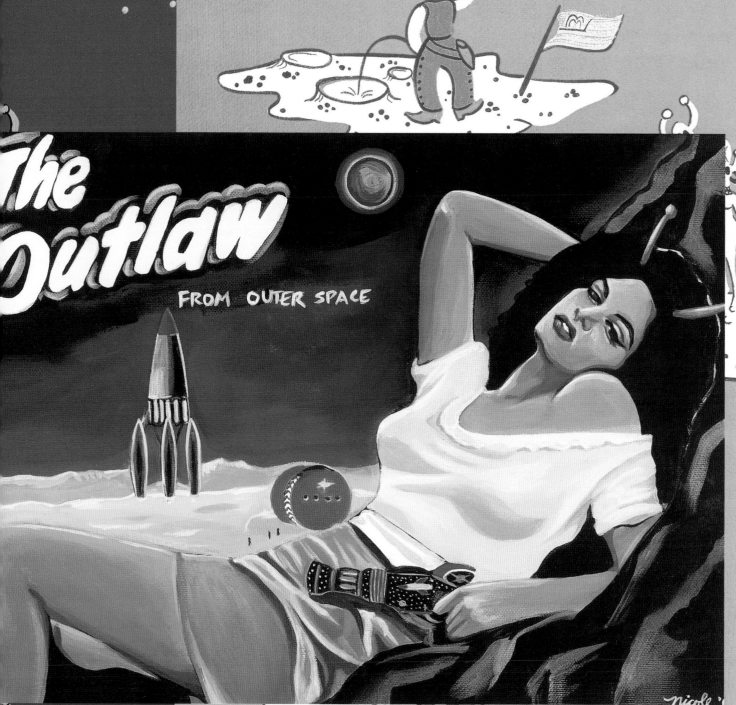

Nicole Steen "The Outlaw From Outer Space"
14" x 10" Acrylic on Canvas, 2002

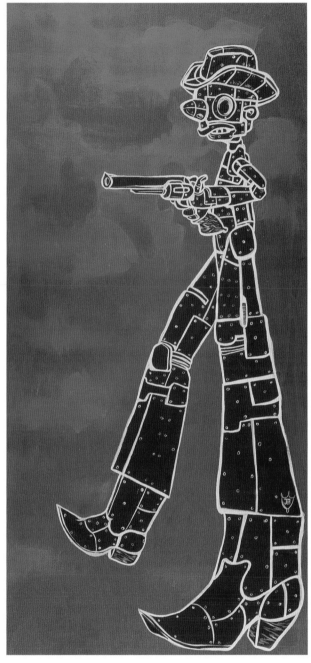

Josh Berkowitz "Reservations"
2(12" x 24") Gouache and Acrylic on Wood, 2002

Mario Martinez "Unti
12" x 15" Oil on Canvas, 2

Christine Karas "Outer Space Kitty Loves Cowboys"
14" x 18" Acrylic on Canvas, 2002

Megan Besmirched "Stranded"
17" x 19" Acrylic on Canvas and Molded Resin, 2002

Kim Scott "Skinny Dipping at Retribution Creek"
30.5" x 36" Oil on Canvas, 2002

Stacy Lande "The Big Bang"
19" x 24" Acrylic on Wood, 2002

abel Samaras "Besame Mucho"
" x 12" Oil on Wood, 2002

Todd Schorr "Hiawatha Encounters the Flying Purple People Eater"
14" x 18" Acrylic on Canvas, 2002

Charles Glaubitz "Kid Manifestdestiny"
65" x 28.5" Mixed Media, 2002

Jeff Soto "Complete Domination"
30" x 12" Acrylic on wood, 2002

Bruce Gossett "Bulleto Verde"
23" x 30" Acrylic on Wood, 2002

Skinner "Space Cocaine"
48" x 24" Acrylic on Wood, 2002

Sean Stepanoff "Lonesome Cowboy"
14.5" x 21.5" Acrylic on Wood, 2002

Joe Leonard "Untitled"
48" x 24" Acrylic on Canvas, 2002

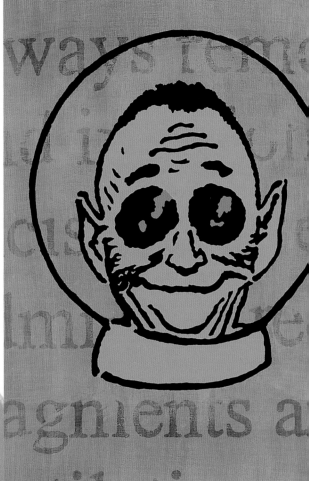

Matthew James "Everyone Loves Barbeque"
3(22" x 30") Acrylic on Canvas, 2002

Jorge R. Gutierrez "Astroboy Bandito"
8" x 10" Acrylic on Wood, 2002

DX "Super Intelligent Beans"
8" x 10" Acrylic on Canvas Board, 2002

Mr. Lucky "Terrible/Beautiful"
48" x 36" Oil on Canvas, 2002

Richard Sala "Stranger in Town"
11" x 14" Watercolor and Ink, 2002

Troy Cook "Git Along Lil Doggie"
60" x 36" Acrylic on Canvas, 2002

Mitch O'Connell "Kid's Today"
25.5" x 11.25" Gouache, 2002

Sky and Sonny J. "Who Was That Black-Faced Man?"
7" x 7" Mixed Media, 2002

Sky and Sonny J. "Little Man"
7.25" x 5.75" Mixed Media, 2002

Sky and Sonny J. "Totally Flip"
5.5" x 7.25" Mixed Media, 2002

Sky and Sonny J. "Smoke Signals"
10.25" x 7.25" Mixed Media, 2002

Sky and Sonny J. "And How"
9.25" x 7.25" Mixed Media, 2002

Dave Cooper "Riding Bareback on the Planet of Giant Naked Ladies"
18" x 18" Oil on Canvas, 2002

Winston Smith "Cowgirlettes in Space"
10" x 10" Montage, 2002

Martin Ontiveros "Vaya Con Dios"
18" x 18" Acrylic on Wood, 2002

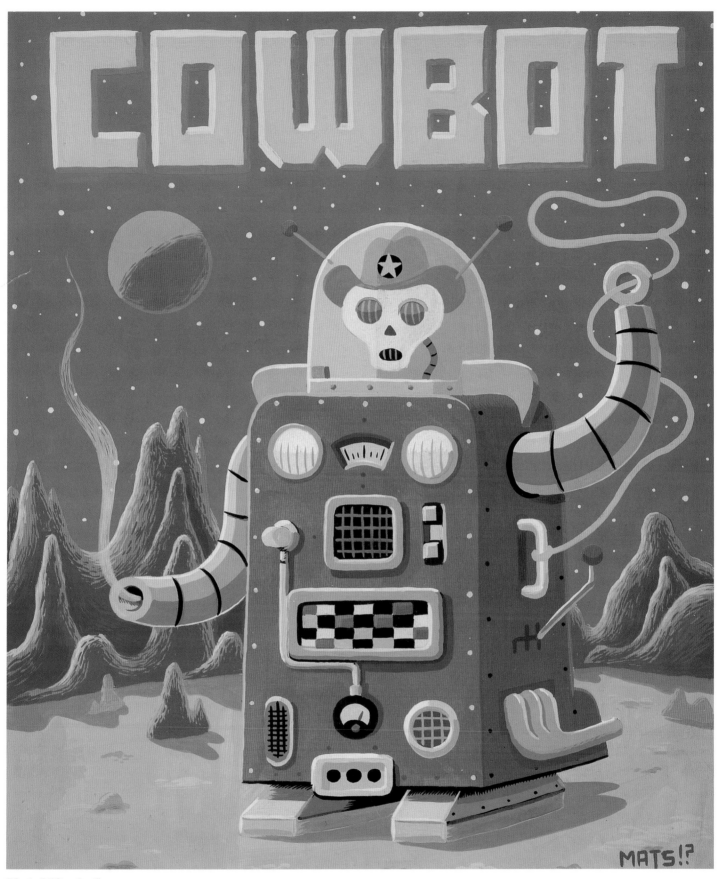

Mats! "Cowbot"
8.5" x 14" Acrylic on Paper, 2002

Diego Mannino "Triumph Of Chief Iron Tail"
16.25" x 20.25" Acrylic on Board, 2002

Brian Hutflies "What The" (Somewherein Nevada)
18" x 24" Acrylic on Panel, 2002

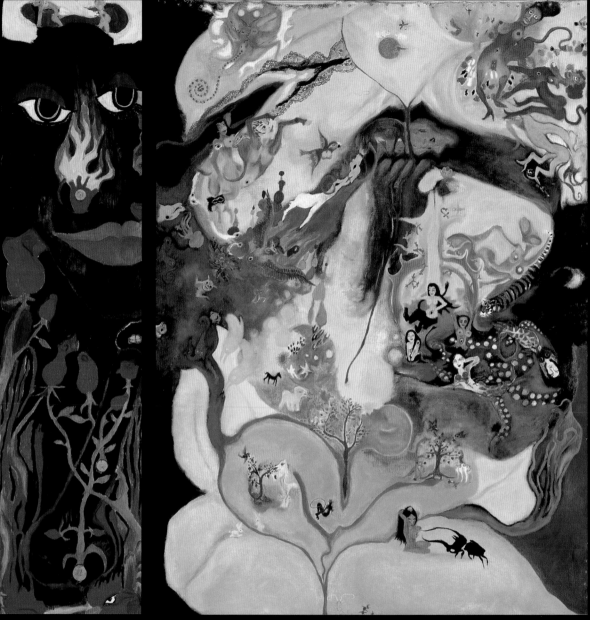
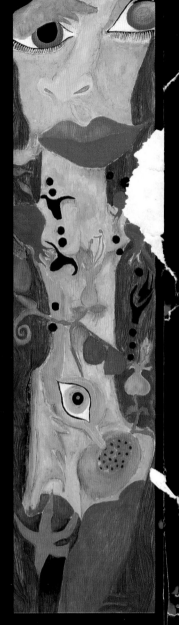

Anastasia Schipani "Somewhere Out West"
58" x 48" Oil on Linen, 2002

Julie Pavlowski "From Campfires to Rocket Fuel"
16" x 20" Mixed Media, 2002

Darren Merinuk "Goonsmoke"
9.75" x 17" Acrylic on Paper, 2002

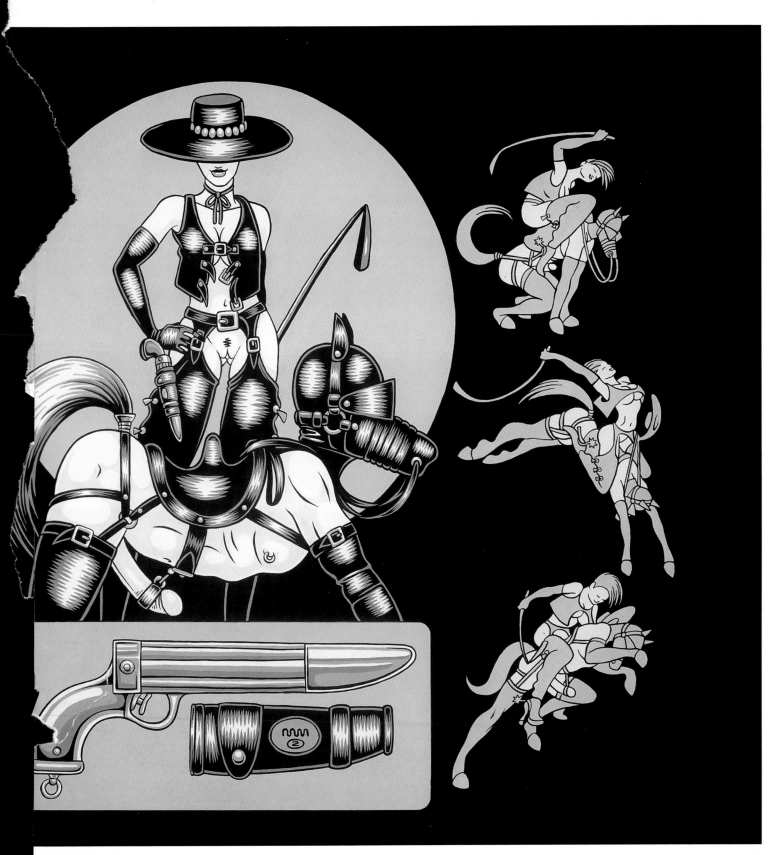

Michael Manning "Lo-Grav Rider and Mount"
17" x 14" Acrylic, Ink, Pencil, on Board, 2002

Pamela Hobbs "Get Lucky"
35" x 60" Oil on Leather, 2002

Chick Fontaine "The Exodus of St. Dypthia"
2(5" x 9") Mixed Media, 2002

Clayton Bailey "Dueling Ray Guns #72 - #73"
19" x 16" x 4" Aluminum, Titanium, Brass, Stainless Steel, Die Cast Metal, Wood, Cork, 1999

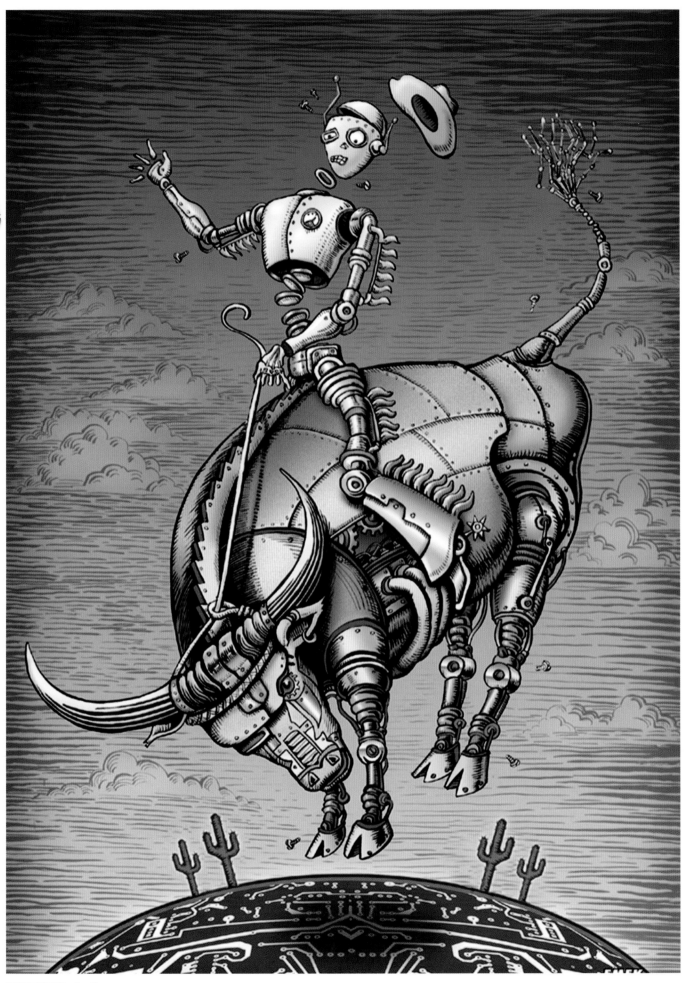

EMEK "Rodeo"
14" x 18" Digital Offset of a Pen and Ink Drawing, 2002

Ludovic Joffrain "Lilas and Her Martian Pal In An Earthling Garden On Mars"
10" x 14" Pen and Ink, 2002

Ludovic Joffrain (Title Untranslated: Martian)
10" x 14" Pen and Ink, 2002

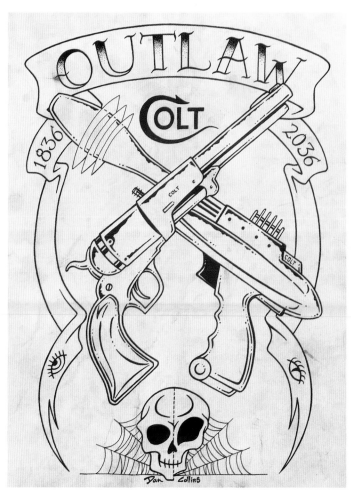

Spain Rodriguez "Mara Mistress of the Void"
10.5" x 14" Pen and Ink on Paper, 2002

Dan Collins "Outlaw"
12" x 16" Indian Ink on Parchment, 2002

KRK Ryden "Visit to the Planet Horn-E/2"
8.5" x 11" Pen and Ink, 1980-2002

Todd Schorr "The Old Prospector Has A Vision Of Green Indians"
30" x 24" Acrylic on Canvas, 1994

Todd Schorr "The Resurrection"
34" x 26" Acrylic on Canvas, 1995

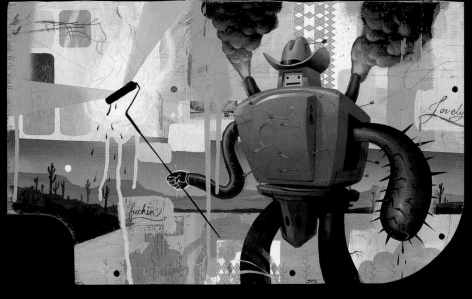

Mark Ryden "Shapeshifter"
18" x 18" Acrylic on Wood, 1999

Jeff Soto "Fuckin' Lovely"
22" x 13" Acrylic, Mixed Media on Wood, 2002

Todd Schorr "Eyewitness To The Cattle Mutilation"
60" x 48" Acrylic on Canvas, 1993

Thank You

MANY THANKS TO ALL THE SPECIAL PEOPLE WHO HELPED WITH THIS PROJECT, AND TO ALL THE ARTISTS WHO PUT THEIR HEART AND SOUL, SWEAT AND BLOOD INTO THE WORK. I ESPECIALLY WOULD LIKE TO THANK THE FOLLOWING ANGELS:

Sasha Wingate
Cary Littlefield
Eiming Jung
Gabe Scott
Eric Haller
Cathie Burgyan
Deanna Marconi
Tyrone McCloskey
Jack Perkins
Ludovic Joffrain
Alethea Morrison
Michael Manning
Peter Macchia
Juxtapoz
Joe Leonard

Jim Breazeale
Robert Williams
EMEK
Mission Graphica
KRK Ryden
Tom Wolf
Penny Skwish
Akemi Okamoto
Henry Goldfield
Ron Turner
Renee Gangnath
Lindsey Byrnes
William Haugh
Annie Tucker
John Clute